Plan it

See it

Anticipate it

3 Secrets to goal setting that will give you a bullseye aim & take action.

Tarnya Coley

Plan it. See it. Anticipate it

© Copyright Tarnya Coley 2021
Published by Tarnya Coley Publishing LTD

All rights reserved 2021 Tarnya Coley Publishing LTD

This book is sold subject to the conditions: it is not, by way of trade or otherwise, lent, hired out or otherwise circulated in any form of binding or cover other than that in which it is published. No part of this publication may be reproduced, stored in a retrieval system or transmitted in any form or by any means (electronic, mechanical, photocopying, recording or otherwise) without prior written permission from the Publisher.

Tarnya Coley

GET YOUR FREE GIFT!

To get the best experience with this eBook, I've found that readers who download and use 'Living your potential' are able to implement changes faster and take the next steps needed to get unstuck and chase after their goals.

You can get a copy by visiting: https://tarnya.systeme.io/ebook

To Mum, Dad, Damian, Roshay and Joel.

My biggest supporters.

This Book Is For You If:

- ❖ You want to stop running up and down the field and start scoring.

- ❖ You need a bullet-proof strategy to achieve your goals.

- ❖ You are looking to take control of your life.

- ❖ You desire to get laser focused.

Foreword

It might be cliché, but life is short. In the blink of an eye, weeks turn into months and months into years. All too often, people find themselves having lived their lives with nothing to show for it. Why is this? Why is it that people live unfulfilling lives until they realise it is too late? This is a question I have asked myself for a long time. If life is so short, why do people waste it?

Everybody has dreams and desires. Since we were kids, we stared at our ceilings hoping to one day be astronauts, rock stars, actresses, and authors. As we matured, these dreams slowly fell to the back of our minds as most of us chose conventional careers. Some of us had families to support and could not afford to chase our dreams. Most of us were told it was impossible. Only a select few of us were able to chase our dreams, and even a smaller selection actually succeeded. Once again, why is this?

Some people are simply dealt poor hands, and there are other in-depth answers to this question. But I think it all stems from one source: people do not know what they are truly capable of. We can all accomplish whatever we put our minds to, but the way we approach our dreams is where we either succeed or come crashing down. Learning to set goals in every walk of life can be the missing piece to the puzzle of success.

Plan It, See It, Anticipate It takes the idea of setting life goals and runs with it. There is a major difference between dreaming wild fantasies and setting meaningful goals, and it is often the deciding factor to success. Tarnya Coley not only lays out a template to set goals the best way possible but does so from personal experience. I have witnessed the power of setting strong goals and know that a determined human mind cannot be stopped. There is no greater testament to this than the author of this book, Tarnya Coley.

I first met Tarnya last year when she joined my 6-month Mastermind program, and I instantly realised how special of a person she is. Throughout the process, she showed initiative and took massive action. Tarnya applied this action, and truly shined while she progressed to triumph. What makes her so successful is how she can separate her past from the present. Tarnya does not let old paradigms and habits drag her down as she strives towards her goals.

There are three main battles in the war for success. The first revolves around creativity and dreaming big. If you can dream it, you can do it, and beginning with huge ambitions will get you started on the road to happiness. The second battle, as Tarnya explains best in this very book, is goal setting. This can be a daunting task, but it is a crucial step if you wish to succeed. The third, and in my opinion the most important step, is your mindset.

Visualisation can make or break the chase of your dreams. Even if you have done everything right, set perfect goals, and developed a masterful plan, your goals will not be achieved unless you believe you can do it. Changing your mindset to fully commit is difficult and scary. Of course, Tarnya knows this just as well as I do and has provided an incredible guide and formula for making that switch in your head.

Hopefully, I have done my job convincing you to read on, but now I want to motivate you. All of this information is fine and dandy, but life is never fair. The cards we are dealt both at birth and in our lifetimes differ so much from person to person. Even with all the steps laid out in front of us, it can feel impossible to ever break the current cycle.

Trust me, I have been there. I am no stranger to hardship and challenges. But we only have one life to live, so why not take a chance? Reaching your goals won't be easy, and it may take uncomfortable sacrifices along the way. But the feeling of accomplishing what you set out to do is unmatched and truly makes life worth living.

It doesn't matter if you're young or old either, there's always time to chase your dreams. At 66 years old, Colonel Sanders was sleeping in the back of his car before franchising his world-famous chicken recipe. Julia Child didn't release her first cookbook until she was 50 years old, and Vera Wang was 41 when she opened her first bridal boutique.

The moral of the story is that nothing can stop you on your path to greatness.

Your greatness will be different from my greatness. And your greatness will be different from your neighbour's greatness. That's what makes us unique. Maybe your goals are huge, and you aspire to run a Fortune 500 company or sell out stadiums. They could be as small as learning to play guitar or speak French. Every single goal, big or small, is just as important to your happiness. Whatever your heart desires, set out and accomplish it, and become the greatest version of yourself you possibly can.

When reading *Plan It, See It, Anticipate It*, I very quickly noticed how it can transform lives. Tarnya has beautifully described a process that so few people have actually completed and has broken it down into simple steps that only she could. I wish that I had this book when I first started on my journey and truly hope that others will see it just as I do.

My last word of advice: open yourself up to your potential. Only you can limit what you can accomplish, so open your mind. Open it to this book and to its ideas. Your brain is your greatest foe.

But that's enough of me. Take a dive into the book, and learn how to truly demolish your hurdles, reach your goals, and find your greatness.

All of the best in your journeys ahead,

Jon Talarico- High Performance Results Coach

Contents

FOREWORD

INTRODUCTION

    Learn to set goals for success. 1

CHAPTER 1: PLAN IT 5

    What's the big deal about goal setting?.. 5
    Tips on planning your goals. 12
    SMART goals 15
    Change the Plan, But The Goal Remains The Same. 18
    Chunk Down Your Goals... 19
    Affirmations for goal setting... 21

CHAPTER 2: SEE IT 26

    Create a vision for your life. 26
    Overcoming Obstacles 29

CHAPTER 3: ANTICIPATE IT 34

    Believe & Succeed 34
    Reject and replace.. 36

CHAPTER 4: WINNING MINDSET FOR SUCCESS.............................44

    SUCCESS Mindset Formula... 45

    Take Action Today 60
    For the Future 65
    Last Word 69
    Craving more? 70
    About the Author 72

Introduction

Learn to set goals for success.

"A goal without a plan is just a wish"

- Antoine de Saint-Exupéry.

Research suggests that 92% of people don't achieve their goals.[1] That is because they are unclear of what they want and have no coherent plan of action.

If you are serious about goal setting and taking action, continue reading this book. You will learn how to be in the eight percent of those that achieve their goals and win every single time.

A vision without goals is useless. Goals give us a 'bullseye' target – something to aim at and keep us focused on the things that really matter. But having too many goals or vague ones can be just as bad as having none!

---

[1] 'Productivity' by Marcel Schwantes 2016.

No more missing the mark; instead, become a master at setting precise, actionable goals. This book will show you how to apply the three steps for goal setting, which include:

- Setting SMART and actionable goals.
- Taking immediate action towards achieving your goals.
- Creating a crystal-clear vision.
- Measuring and reviewing your progress.
- Mastering your mindset.

I have provided templates in this book so you can apply what you learn. Now is the time to set goals so that you can achieve the results you desire! 'Plan it. See it. Anticipate it' (the PSA method) is focused on goal setting and getting the desired outcome. I designed this method because I am driven to improve people's lives – people who are missing the mark and not achieving their goals.

No more setting goals and never following through, citing various reasons why you have not achieved your goals. Eric Worre once said, *"what is bigger, your dreams or your excuses?"*

It's time to follow through on your goals and see them come to fruition. I used the PSA method to write my bestselling book 'Open Doors' in six weeks. The PSA method is a Goal Positioning System aimed to help you set, aim, and fire.

I have helped hundreds of individuals globally to fine-tune their vision, set goals, and achieve what they desire. I encourage others to have a plan for their lives. Where are you going? How will you get there? These are key questions to ask yourself as you embark on setting goals for your life, business, job or family.

What is stopping you from going after what you want? Fear, doubt, lack of confidence, yourself? Serve notice to those negative thoughts and feelings today. Get out of your own way and thrive. Strolling to your goals is not an option. You have the potential inside of you - unleash it, and you will be unstoppable.

I used to be a sleeping lion, not utilising my gifts and talents. Not going after what I really wanted and playing small. That was because I had limited vision. My plans were vague and not specific. I didn't believe that I could achieve what I really wanted. I was living life on a default setting.

"If you aim at nothing, you will hit it every time."

Zig Ziglar.

There came a point in my life when I woke up and realised, I *have* potential. No more sleeping lions, playtime is over. I made a choice to get serious about what I wanted in life. Like the lion chases its prey, I chased after what I wanted. Rewriting the script of my life was now more important than being a spectator. No longer watching others achieving their goals and living life with purpose. I had a made-up mind and was determined to be a goal-getter. You have to start somewhere to get somewhere. Be focused, fearless and unstoppable.

If you apply the secrets that are exposed in this book, you will have a road map for your goals and hit the bullseye for achieving them.

Let us embark together on your journey to setting clear goals, taking action and developing a mindset for success.

PLAN IT. SEE IT. ANTICPATE IT

Chapter 1

Plan it

What's the big deal about goal setting?

"The trouble with not having a goal is that you can spend your life running up and down the field and never score."

- Bill Copeland.

When embarking on a journey, planning is essential and integral to any part of the process. Planning is setting out what you need to do in order to carry something out. Planning your goals is key to getting to where you need to be. Look at it as a GPS, Goal Positioning System. In order to get somewhere, you need to have a plan. Living your life by design is what we were born to do, this is non-negotiable. Not living on the default setting.

Goals are ideas of the future or desired result that you envision, plan and commit to achieve. Setting goals is the first step to turning the invisible into the visible. Decide today that you will be a goal-getter and turn your dream into reality.

There are two types of people in life. There are people who let life simply happen to them; following the crowd, uncertain what direction to take, largely because of fear. They let things happen and blame others or situations for not achieving their goals. These people respond to life and let life dictate their choices. This is called living life on a default setting.

However, there are other people that make plans and set goals. Most importantly, they take action in order to achieve their purpose in life. They see opportunities and clutch them with both hands and run with them. Waiting for the perfect time and conditions is something they *don't* do. They go for it and make it happen. Having a plan of action and being purposeful is how they live their lives.

Setting goals gives your life direction and boosts your motivation and self-confidence. It is the foundation for the things you want to accomplish. Without a concrete foundation, you'll lose focus on your end goals. Knowing what to do is not the issue, committing to it is the problem.

Sometimes we can lack the correct structures to support the behavioural changes our life goals require. There needs to be commitment, consistency and calmness.

It is so easy to fall into the bad habits that lead to a life lived by default. Therefore, it is important to have clarity on your goals and the direction that you want to take. Bob Proctor teaches the 'Knowing/ Doing Gap'. We have to be aware of the unhealthy habits that we have, because it helps to close the gap of what I know and what I do. Sometimes people can do things that they do not want to do, that is why they get the results they do not want to get.

> *"Everything in your life is a reflection of a choice you have made. If you want a different result, make a different choice."*
>
> **- Anonymous.**

Using myself as an example: Some time ago I realised that I needed to demand more out of myself. Playing small was not doing me any favours. I wasn't living to my full potential. A change had to be made in order to achieve real transformation. If you want to see a different result, you have to do things differently. I got serious about my life and the direction I wanted to go. The PSA method helped me get unstuck and reach my goals so I can make a greater impact. I created a plan and got clear on what I wanted. Then I visualised where I was going and believed that I would achieve my life's purpose.

In order to achieve your goals, assess where you are right now. Where do you want to be a year from now? Look at yourself holistically, in the physical, intellectual, emotional, social and spiritual sense.

Physical- Your physical well-being is important for your overall health. Do you want to get fitter, eat healthier? Do you need to practice more self-care? Asking yourself these questions will allow you to pin-point what you need to work on.

Intellectual- Investing in your personal development is a lifelong process. You must always grow, and always be learning. As the bible says, *"an intelligent heart gains knowledge, and the ear of the wise seeks knowledge."* - Proverbs 18:15. Be dedicated to learning, growing, and being the best you can be. Learning never exhausts the mind. What are you doing to be always growing and always learning?

Emotional- Your emotional health is the positive sense of well-being which permits individuals to function in society and meet the stresses of everyday life.

Social- Connecting with family and friends allows us to build better relationships. It is crucial to reach out when you need support or guidance. Studies have shown that having supportive relationships is a strong protective factor against mental illnesses and helps to increase our mental well-being.

We need to have supportive relationships and be a listening ear to others. Social health is your ability to form satisfying interpersonal relationships with others. It also relates to your ability to adapt comfortably to different social situations and act appropriately in a variety of settings.

Spiritual- Spiritual well-being is having compassion, the capacity for love and forgiveness, unselfishness, joy, and fulfilment. Your religious faith, values, beliefs, principles, and morals define your spirituality. Do you need to re-align with your core values?

Plan it. See it. Anticipate it

This reflective exercise will allow you to see where you are *now* and where you want to go.

List the goals that you want to achieve for each heading.

REFLECTIVE EXERCISE

PHYSICAL
_____
_____
_____
_____

INTELLECTUAL
_____
_____
_____
_____

EMOTIONAL
_____
_____
_____
_____

Plan it. See it. Anticipate it

REFLECTIVE EXERCISE

SOCIAL

SPIRITUAL

NOTES

Now that you have assessed where you are and where you want to be, here are some tips on planning your goals. At the end of this chapter there are worksheets for you to plan the life of your dreams.

Tips on planning your goals.

1. Write down your goals. It sounds simple, but this is part of achieving your goals. There is power in the pen. If you are not used to writing your goals down, try it. Write down what you want. It is like making a contract with yourself. This is not the time to be vague, get clear on what you want. Then speak your goals out loud, morning and night. Scientists say that people who write down their goals are 42% more likely to achieve them than people who don't write them down. Just on that evidence alone, I encourage you to write your goals down. *"Write the vision. And make it plain on tablets, that he may run who reads it."* - Habakkuk 2:2.

Now that you have written your goals down, ask yourself: What is your 'why' for each goal that you have set yourself? When your 'why' is strong enough, it will motivate and inspire you to work hard to achieve it. A 'just because' goal will not propel you forward. Where there is not a strong enough 'why', you are less likely to achieve your goals.

When I left my career of 15 years as a lecturer, I reached a point where I knew there was more for me to do. There was a powerful reason why I was leaving my security and safe job. I wanted to spend more time with my family. I wanted to stop missing out on my children's school productions. I took the job home with me and was working most weekends, burning the candle at both ends. I vividly remember frantically looking for my car keys one morning. I thought, if I don't find them now, I'm going to be extremely late for work. Moments later I found them, in the ignition of my car, left there overnight.

My goodness, it dawned on me, I was exhausted, overworked and stressed. I had to make a choice: stay in the job and put up with my work situation. Just put up and shut up and continue to daydream about escaping. Or leave and pursue my life's purpose. I made a decisive decision and turned my back on my career. My well-being was more important. And so I embarked on a journey to live my purpose. What is your 'why'?

2. Surround yourself with like-minded people. You become like those who you keep close. Evaluate your friendship groups, who do you have around you? The friends that you have, do you strive to be like them, do you respect and regard them in high esteem? It is time to take an inventory of those around you. Surround yourself with positive people who are going to push you to your greatness. Who is in your circle?

3. Practice discipline. *"Discipline is the bridge between goals and achievement. Discipline creates habits, habits make routines, and routines become who you are daily."* - Jim Rohn.

Being disciplined is the ability to do what you should be doing. Think about the long-term gain as opposed to the immediate. It will give you direction and avoid distraction by seeing what needs to be completed. With discipline, anything is possible. You will not achieve your goals if you are continually in a state of 'can't be bothered'. Self-discipline gives you the power to stick to your decisions and follow them through, without changing your mind, and is one of the important requirements for achieving goals.

4. Take action. Just do it. Verbalising your goals is not enough. Take productive action steps towards what you want to do. Write down what you need to do in order to fulfil your goals. Always follow through and be consistent. Each day take one step that will lead you to your desired goals.

These tips will help you live life by design, not by default. More will discussed on taking action further in the book.

5. Be accountable. Holding yourself accountable to yourself will not bring about masses of results. Nobody knows what you are working on, and you can move your goals if you have not achieved them. You need to have a healthy perspective from others and wise judgement. Find yourself an accountability partner with whom you can hold each other accountable. Or hire a coach, invest in yourself, because you are worth the investment. You can't see the full picture when you're in the frame. A coach will help you to have those lightbulbs and 'aha' moments.

They will tell you what you need to hear, not what you want to hear. They will give you a vision of yourself far beyond where you are right now. This type of support will help you immensely because it will help you stay committed. Having that extra support will only help you take action. A year from now you'll wish you had started today.

6. Celebrate your wins. Celebrating your wins is essential as it helps you build confidence. Take the time to reflect on your achievements before moving on to the next goal. When you celebrate your wins, it allows you to think in a more positive way.

It will also help build momentum. *If I achieve this goal, I know I can achieve the next goal.* This will attract more success and set you up with motivation for moving forward towards your next goal with enthusiasm.

SMART goals

Having SMART goals enables you to be crystal clear on setting effective goals and evaluating regularly where you are in terms of achieving them.

Your goal must be **Specific.** What do you want to achieve? Why do you want to achieve it?

A good friend of mine, Jannette Barrett puts it this way: What do you want? What don't you want? What have you got? Now then, be decisive!

Measurable- How will you measure your goal? How will you know when you have reached your goal?

Achievable- How will you achieve your goal? What steps do you need to take to get there?

Realistic- Is your goal realistic? What resources do you need to achieve it?

Timely- Do you have a time when you will achieve your goal?
Let me take this a step further. You should also **evaluate** and **re-adjust** your goals. Each month, develop a healthy habit of evaluating and reviewing your goals to help you stay on track. Evaluate and review your goals regularly because you want to measure the impact. Using 'The simple way to get motivated goal planner' will assist you with this step.

Develop a weekly action plan which will show you exactly what you need to do each day. Think about what you need to do today to move you closer to your goals and then get started. Commit to achieving your goal and don't let anything stand in the way! Make a commitment to your commitments.

Fill in the goals template on the next page. This is an opportunity for you to put into practice what you have just read. Do not rush this process. Take some dedicated time to go through the template. This is your life plan, so don't rush, and remember you can make adjustments as you go along.

Plan it. See it. Anticipate it

Use the SMARTER plan to guide you to ensure that your goal is specific.

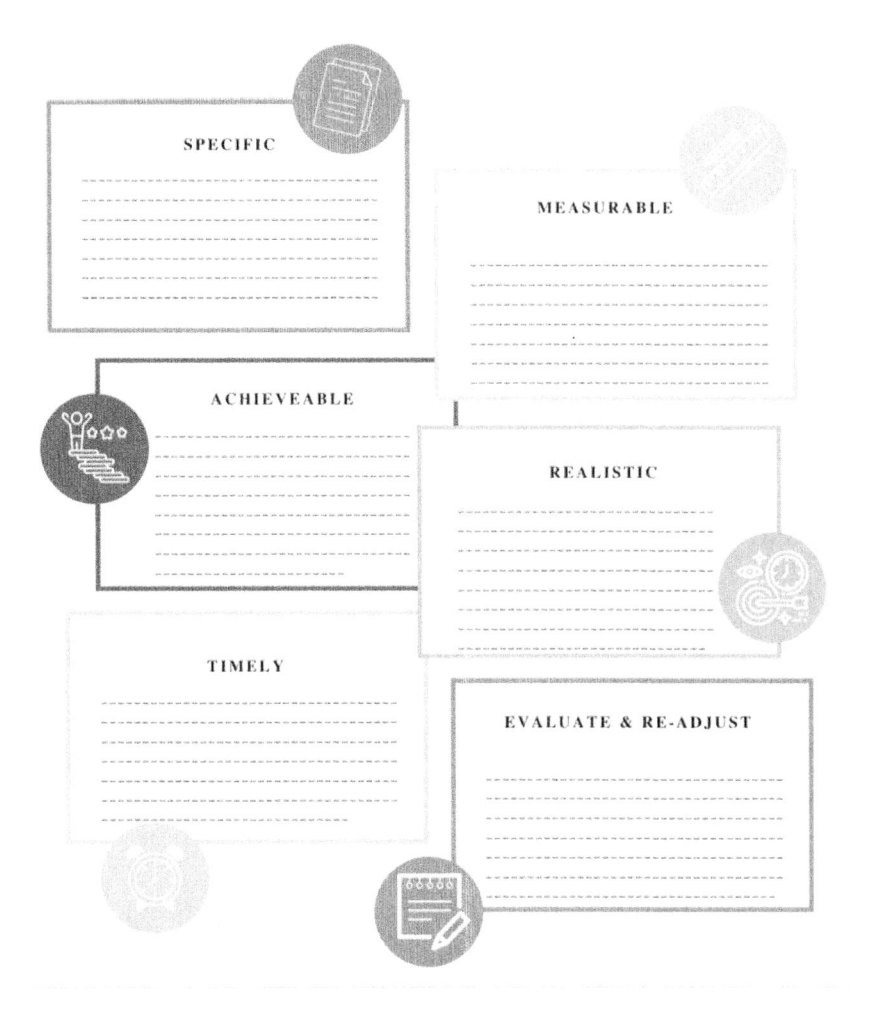

SPECIFIC

MEASURABLE

ACHIEVEABLE

REALISTIC

TIMELY

EVALUATE & RE-ADJUST

Change the Plan, But The Goal Remains The Same.

I recall when a client of mine had a moment in her life when she thought: I want to do more with my life. She felt stuck and had a strong desire to move forward. On the one hand she wanted to leave her job as a teacher, in order to run her own business. But she felt trapped by the feelings of self-doubt, fear of failure and negative thinking. To take action felt terrifying, but to do nothing felt worse.

Together, we came up with a plan of action. I explained the PSA method and how it would benefit her. She decided to take a chance on herself. First, I asked her, what is it you really want? It was apparent to see she had comprehensive plans. We wrote her goals down. Then we broke them down into manageable steps. We now had a bullet-proof action plan. She was accountable to me each step of the way. Having this structure in place allowed her to see that it was possible for her to achieve her goals.

Each time we meet, she was making massive leaps and grew in confidence. Those negative feelings were fading. She became unstoppable because she believed that it would happen. She put in the time and effort to bring about what she wanted. Since implementing those steps, she has now started her own business and is thriving.

Today is the day you will work on you and what you want to accomplish. No more playing average, sitting on the side-lines watching others and being a spectator. Decide to chase after your goals and dreams. Remember, planning is an integral part of the process.

Chunk Down Your Goals

Having a big, ambitious goal is absolutely fine. But sometimes we delay or put off our goals because we become overwhelmed. Chunking down your ideas will help you break down your goals so they become more manageable. Break down your goals into long- medium- and short-term goals. Write your thoughts in the short-medium-long term planning worksheet.

I like to work backwards when working on my goals. This has helped me immensely to achieve them. Ask yourself these important questions, they will help you to nail down your goal:

- What do I want to achieve a year from now?
- What do I need to achieve in one to three months?
- What do I need to achieve in four to six months?
- What do I need to achieve in seven to twelve months?

Start with your long-term goals and work backwards.

Short-Medium-Long term target planning

SMALL

MEDIUIM

LONG

Affirmations for goal setting

Affirmations for goal setting will help you keep your goals at the forefront of your mind. Regularly using goal affirmations will help to condition your mind to help you achieve the goals you have set. Verbalising your affirmations can help you overcome self-sabotage and negative thoughts. When you repeat them often, and believe them, you can make positive changes. Plant those seeds of I AM and I CAN.

- I can do anything I put my mind to.
- I have faith in myself and in my abilities.
- I have what it takes to reach my goals.
- I can handle anything that comes my way.
- Great strength lies within me at all times.
- I have the courage to keep going.
- I have the courage to walk my own path and follow my dreams.
- I can do anything I set my mind to do.
- I will not allow the opinions of others deter me.
- I will do something each day towards my goals.

PLAN IT
Goal setting template

My goal (Be specific)

Why do you want to achieve that goal?

Why do you want to achieve this goal now?

If you do not achieve this goal what are the consequences?

How will you measure your goal?

PLAN IT
Goal setting template

What resources do I need to achieve my goal?

Is your goal realistic?

What date do I want to achieve it by?

Declaration: I am committed to achieving my goal, and I will not let anything stand in my way!

Take action on this step before you move on!

Action steps

1. Always have a plan of action as this will help you get to your destination. Remember, there will be distractions along the way. But you have now developed your road map just in case of eventualities.
2. Use the tools that have been provided to set effective goals so you can hit the bullseye.
3. Ensure that your goals are specific, measurable, achievable realistic and timely. Regularly evaluate and re-adjust your goals.
4. Make sure you verbalise your affirmations to bring your goals into alignment.

Plan it. See it. Anticipate it

My Notes

PLAN IT. SEE IT. ANTICIPATE IT

Chapter 2

See it

Create a vision for your life.

"A vision without action is merely a dream. Action without vision just passes the time. Vision with action can change the world."

- Joel Arthur Barker.

A common misconception is that seeing is believing. This is not accurate. We can't see the air, yet we know it is all around, so does that mean the air does not exist? We have to have faith in what we want to see. *"Without vision the people perish…"* - Proverbs 29:18.

We need a vision of our future so we can plan. In order to see things come to pass, you need to turn your vision into a reality.

Now that you have your goal worked out and written down, start planning how you will get there. You have to be able to see where you are going if you want to reach the correct destination. It is time to visualise the journey ahead. Seeing is all about vision. Many people have sight, but no vision. Keep your eyes open and create a vision for your life.

Have you heard the term 'eagle eye'? Eagles are blessed with remarkable 20/5 vision. Their vision is extremely sharp. They are clear on where they are going, and they soar high. Be like the eagle, have crystal clear vision and soar high above your circumstances and situations.

Eagles can soar high because they travel light. They do not carry baggage. Just like the eagle, you have to travel light. If not, the road you are travelling, called life, will be a very intensive journey. Take action on your vision, today. The cost of your vision is perseverance and maintaining the vision is endurance.

Blindness can leave you exposed and unsure where you are, or where you are heading. Vision loss can impact you. You may have given up on your dream, thinking that it may never happen. The negative self-talk starts, *I'm too old, I don't have all the skills*; the list goes on. Then you may completely lose sight of where you are, and want to revert to the default setting. This can cause a deterioration in yourself. The comfort zone is a place of familiarity and ease, yet nothing grows in comfort zones. You can become overwhelmed and frightened. The complete loss or the deterioration of existing eyesight can feel frightening and overwhelming, leaving those affected to wonder about their life.

In my earlier years, I suffered from 'possibility blindness'. Echoes of my past would often play on my mind. I was going through life aimlessly, and life was meaningless. Being in this mode was not baring any fruit and it wasn't showing results. In order for me to change, I had to take positive steps. I needed to grab a hold of the vision for my life and get clear on what I wanted. I realised I was getting in my own way. Many things shifted in my life when I realised what I wanted to do, so I created a clear vision, focused and gained clarity.

Carol Bryant stated that, "there are three types of people: those who make things happen, those who watch things happen, and those who wonder what happened". Be the person who makes things happen. You have a goal, and you can see where you are going. Keep moving forward until you get there.

Vision enables you to see where you are going. It gives you focus and direction. Be bold enough to pursue your goals that are in alignment with that vision. Do not pursue your vision in the expectation and views of others. Create a large vision, vison defines your passion and purpose and creates the life we choose to live.

Be aware that other people can be a stumbling block to your vision. Remember, you have control over your life, do not give your control to others. When people are not in alignment with what you do, or do not understand, it can take you off course.

Are you impending your own vision, whether it is because of fear, self-doubt, lack of confidence? If so, it is imperative to develop strategies to overcome the negativity and keep it at bay.

Overcoming Obstacles

On the journey there will be obstacles. Become a problem solver so you can stay on track to succeed. Develop strategies to help you overcome those obstacles. Having control over your life will allow you to make important decisions and feel less overwhelmed, lost and stuck. No, we cannot control everything, but we can control how we respond to situations and the challenges we face.

Yes, the obstacles are there, however you have to navigate your way through. Put on your GPS, Goal Positioning System. This will tell you where you are right now and what lies ahead. Unexpected life events may lurk out in front or behind you. But you have the tools to combat the obstacles and challenges that life presents or throws at you. It is important to design your life.

Plan it. See it. Anticipate it.

Designing a vision board is great way of creating a vision for your life. Let go of what was and have faith in what will be. Visualise that you have already achieved your goal. Believe that it will happen, because it *will*.

Creating a vison board helps you to visualise your goals until they materialise. We think in pictures, for example, when you want to buy a car, you start to imagine the car you want to buy, the colour, driving and parking it outside of your home. It is exactly the same as visualising your goals.

Visualise that you have already achieved your goal. Then, think about how it feels. When you've written this down, then you have your vision board with the visualisation of your goals and how you will achieve them. Now that you have a visualisation of what your goals are and what's it going to be like when you achieve them, you've got an emotional connection with your goals. You're imprinting that vision to your subconscious mind because your subconscious mind doesn't know the difference between reality and visualisation. This is why it's important to align your subconscious mind with the outcomes that you want to see.

Feeling lost in her negative thoughts and drowning in her emotions was how my client felt. She was in a place where she felt despair, no vision for the future. Panic would often set in, unsure what lay ahead. She felt she was losing her vision, being told that her dreams were not possible. Something within her said, you can make it, keep on going. It is possible. She held on to that inner feeling and plucked up the courage to believe again. She believed in her abilities to achieve her goals. Now she has a vision of where she is going.

Use the vision board template and design your life. You can update your board when you have achieved your one of your goals and replace it with another goal.

Plan it. See it. Anticipate it

VISION BOARD
THE BEST IS YET TO COME!

FAVORITE QUOTE

PERSONAL/ FAMILY

WORK/ BUSINESS

DAILY 'MUST DO'S'

Tarnya Coley
Believe I Can

Action Steps

1. Create a larger vision for a life you desire.
2. Have a strategy on how to overcome your obstacles.
3. Become a problem solver so you focus on where you are going.
4. Design a vision board to visualise until it materialises.

Plan it. See it. Anticipate it

My Notes

PLAN IT. SEE IT. ANTICIPATE IT

Chapter 3

Anticipate it

Believe & Succeed

*"The future belongs to those who **believe** in the beauty of their dreams."*

- Eleanor Roosevelt.

Anticipation is waiting in expectation, knowing it *will* happen. When you have that determined mindset, you know that anything is possible. Believing in what you want to achieve is key to seeing what you want to see come true. Believing is accepting that something is true, *"for we live by faith, not by sight."* - 2 Corinthians 5:7.

If you don't believe that what you want will happen, you may have a hard time making things occur because you don't have the belief. I have heard it said that you have to borrow the belief of others sometimes until you believe it will happen for you.

Hold the vision; it all starts with you. Believing that your goals will happen is a lifetime commitment and you have to put in the hard work.

In order for things to take place you must be ready for success and you have to be consistent in working on your goals and keep 'showing up'. Be strong-minded and persevere. A great analogy by Jim Watkins: "a river does not break through the rock because of its power, but because of its determination". You are capable of doing great things, because you have unlimited potential. You have the ability to have more and to be more than you are right now.

Reflecting on my life, there have been times when I just wanted to quit. I didn't believe in myself, or my abilities. I felt I wasn't good enough and inadequate. Fear was the voice that would scream the loudest. The fear of failure was something that gripped me, I just wanted to succeed. I had to remind myself that failure is ok. And ask myself, what life lesson will I learn from this. Looking at it from that perspective gave me the courage to keep believing until I succeeded. I had to continually tell myself that I *can* do it.

Have you considered what you need to do to get the job done? Perseverance and determination are the driving force, your motivator to keep going. You will not always feel like it. Focus on the outcome, not the obstacle. There will always be setbacks, but you have to make a comeback.

When obstacles occur, learn from what has happened. I heard someone once say, don't allow a setback to make you to sit back, you have to make a come-back. Have comeback power.

Focus on where you are going, not where you are right now. Looking down and walking forwards, your posture gives the impression of defeat and discouragement. Adjust your posture and look ahead, position yourself. Plant those seeds of positivity and dig up those weeds.

Reject and replace

The words that we speak have power. When words leave our mouths, we cannot take them back. The negative words we speak to ourselves can be damaging. Today is the day where we become more mindful of our thoughts and what leaves our mouth. Catch yourself speaking and thinking negatively.

Same old thinking, same old results. I received a call from my client, I could hear the excitement in her voice, I didn't know what she wanted to tell me, but I knew it was good news. I smiled, she blurted out, "reject and replace, I am using this method that you have taught me".

Negative thoughts haunted my client, she would often speak in negative ways about herself and she did not believe in her God-given abilities. I would often encourage her to replace the self-destroying words and replace them with life-giving statements. *"There is life and death in the power of the tongue."* - Proverbs 18:21.

At first, it will be difficult to do. You are changing your behaviours and replacing them with new habits. You must practice speaking positively each day until it becomes your lifestyle. There is power in your words. Speak life to yourself and others.

Think and write down all the negative statements that are often said. Then on the opposite side replace them with positive statements. By carrying out this exercise, you are developing a healthy vocabulary. Use the worksheet to carry out this exercise.

REJECT AND REPLACE

REJECT
Negative word

REPLACE
Positive word

I can't do it ┈┈┈>

Doing the minimum will not take you where you want to get to. Negative self-talk and limiting beliefs will not bring the results you want. Change the game and set your sights on things to come. Believe that you will achieve it.

I was born to a teenage mother; she was 16 years-old when she had me. She was told to have me fostered, told to leave home, and her boyfriend left her. Her mess became her message for others to be encouraged. Do not let your start become your end.

Despite my mum's setback, she still had a vision to become a social worker and write a book. She held on to the vision and believed that she would become a social worker. She became the first person in her family to graduate from university and became a social worker. And now, a published author. Many people counted her out, but she believed it would happen. My mum took the steps to complete the book she always wanted to write. I am proud to say my mum did it. Whatever the mind can conceive and believe, it can achieve.

My mum made it happen by enlisting the help of others. The people that supported her to achieve her goals believed that she could do it. She had the attitude of, 'I'm able and I'm willing'. Let this be a reminder, you *can* do it. Are you willing to do whatever it takes to make it happen? Remember, you have unlimited potential. Keep speaking those positive words of affirmation. These are statements directed to reverse self-sabotaging or self-negative talk. Expect it to happen! Focus on the outcome, not the obstacle. Here are some affirmations to help you on your journey to greatness.

These affirmations can help you eliminate something from your life or create something new.

Who are you grateful for? Whether it be your family, friends, neighbours be grateful for those individuals who take the time out to support you. To make you feel more proficient and give you some life hacks that they never had. Be grateful for their guidance, support, and listening ear. Jot down those individuals you are grateful for on the worksheet provided. Make it a part of your morning routine to speak out the names of people you are grateful for. In doing this, you are adapting an attitude of gratitude.

Starting an Attitude of Gratitude

This year, I'm grateful for...

_____
_____
_____
_____
_____
_____
_____
_____
_____
_____
_____
_____
_____
_____
_____
_____
_____

Action steps

1. Decide what you want.
2. Decide what you are prepared to give up to make it happen.
3. Set your mind on it and continue to focus on where you are going.
4. Get to work and do not let anything stand in your way.

My Notes

PLAN IT. SEE IT. ANTICIPATE IT

Chapter 4

Winning mindset for success

In order to achieve your goals, you have to think differently because mindset is key. Your mindset needs shifting.

I recall working on a project; the committee in my mind was telling me that it was not possible for me to achieve what I wanted with the project. Using my toolbox I was able to counteract the negativity with positive words. Working on our minds is a continuous process. *"Be transformed by the renewing of your mind"* - Romans 12:2.

Renewing your mind simply means filling your mind daily by doing the following:

- Reading books which will broaden your mind.
- Listening to positive podcasts forces you to use your imagination and build pictures in your mind.
- Speaking positive affirmations will help to challenge the negative self-talk.
- Start believing that you can control your mindset.

Then, when challenges occur or obstacles arise, your new modus operandi is to see and handle things differently. You have developed a mindset shift, this new perspective changes everything. Your mind is the most valuable asset you have.

Work on your mindset daily, this is non- negotiable. Develop a mindset that looks to solve problems instead of dwelling on them. Having a transformational mindset is necessary for growth.

Developing a winning mindset will help you with motivation. It will inspire you to take action. Once you develop that winning mindset, it changes your outlook, and you will see things differently.

No more of that negative thinking. When you decide to think positively, things change in the direction that you were not expecting.

It is time to change the game. You *can* do this, stay focused and alert. Remain sharp, keep your eyes on the prize, and take one day at a time.

What are you going to do today to create that winning mindset? Remember, this is a continual process. Having a positive mindset is beneficial for your well-being and the key to your success. You can either be a master or slave to your mind. There is no middle ground.

SUCCESS Mindset Formula

Having a powerful, practical action formula is imperative for you to win. This is what you need to use today to change the actions and thought patterns of tomorrow.

Stop That Stinking Thinking

Are you dwelling on 'what ifs?' *What if it doesn't work? What if nobody likes what I'm doing? What if nobody supports me?* Change your language to 'what if it works?' Research suggests that 98% of our self-talk is negative. Focus on the positive things. *"Whatever is true, whatever is honourable, whatever is just, whatever is pure, whatever is lovely, whatever is commendable, if there is any excellence, if there is anything worthy of praise, think about these things."* - Philippians 4:8. Saturate your mind with positivity.

Fortifying your mind is another way to guard your mind from negative influences. Your mind is a special gift. It's your job to reinforce your mind, it's critical. How we think determines how we live our lives. There are so many external situations currently taking place, the pandemic, lack of job security, feeling hopeless. Les Brown often says, *"Be concerned but don't be consumed."*

We need a mind protection plan. By setting up this kind of protection it will make your mind sturdier and extremely difficult to attack. *"Upgrade your thinking, as a man thinketh so is he,"* - Proverbs 23:7.

Have the right application of thought. Think positive and create a positive environment. Upgrade your mind, what you feed your mind becomes your mindset. I challenge you to fortify your mind.

Use A Morning Routine

Set yourself up for success. How do you like to start your day? Having a morning routine will help you to focus and stay on track. Being consistent is the key. Consistency leads to habits. Habits form the action we take every day. Action leads to success. Setting a routine can be a winner for people having great productive days. It is about commencing the day with confidence, peace and a positive attitude. You can then manage things without feeling overwhelmed and feeling constantly anxious.

Be consistent and plan the night before. Establishing a morning routine is non-negotiable.

There are benefits to using a morning routine:
- It helps to set the tone for the day.
- It better allows you to control your schedules rather than your schedules controlling you.
- It reduces stress.
- It helps you to be more productive.

A study performed at the Dominican University of California showed that those who took the time to simply write out their goals were significantly more likely to accomplish them than those who didn't. You can easily apply the same approach to creating new and positive habits. By taking a few minutes to write down what a perfect morning routine would look like, you're increasing your chances of successfully performing them on a more regular basis. Having a morning routine will help you get ready for the day.

Example of a morning routine
- Plan your day the night before.
- Pray/meditate.
- Speak out positive affirmations to overcome self-sabotaging and negative thoughts.
- Attitude of gratitude: write down who and what you are grateful for.
- Read something positive to help you stay focused.
- Listen to a motivational podcast.
- Go for a walk.

What does your morning routine look like?

Cultivate an attitude of gratitude

Practice gratitude daily. Gratitude is strongly and consistently linked with greater happiness. Gratitude helps people to find more positive emotions. It improves your health. Makes you feel less self-centred and helps you to build strong relationships.

Acknowledge the good that you already have in your life - this is the foundation for all abundance. Write down what and who you are grateful for. Even people that help you build your character. Recite a positive quote each morning. Think about what it means to you. This can transform the way you think and view things.

Lend a helping hand to others. Think about who you can reach out to. Using these strategies helps you not focus on the things that steal your joy. Count your blessings, there are many reasons to be happy. You are alive, you're breathing. Be happy. Gratitude gives you the fuel to persevere.

This story is a further way to think about what arises from us, especially in times of stress or disruption:

> *You are holding a cup of coffee when someone comes along and bumps into you or shakes your arm, making you spill your coffee everywhere.*
>
> *Why did you spill the coffee?*
>
> *"Well because someone bumped into me, of course!"*
>
> *Wrong answer.*
>
> *You spilled the coffee because there was coffee in your cup.*
>
> *Had there been tea in the cup, you would have spilled tea.*
>
> *Whatever is inside the cup, is what will spill out.*
>
> *Therefore, when life comes along and shakes you (which WILL happen), whatever is inside you will come out. It's easy to fake it, until you get rattled.*
>
> *So we have to ask ourselves... "what's in my cup?"*

> *When life gets tough, what spills over?*
>
> *Joy, gratefulness, peace and humility?*
>
> *Or anger, bitterness, harsh words and reactions?*
>
> *You choose!*
>
> *Today let's work towards filling our cups with gratitude, forgiveness, joy, words of affirmation, and kindness, gentleness and love for others.*
>
> **Credit: Megan Gooden**

Be thankful, grateful and remember you are truly blessed.

Create a motivation mindset

Build a motivation mindset. Dream it. Do it. Live it. Motivation is the driving force that inspires you to take action in your life.

Know your strengths, this will give you the confidence and the motivation to take action. You will also make smarter choices. Motivation is the key to unlocking your potential.

Find the 'why' behind your goals. You need an empowering WHY. Someone once said what you get by achieving your goals is not as important as what you become by achieving your goals.

Stay hungry and keep the momentum going.

Journal about your goals and write them down.

It's like planting a seed. Don't forget your mind is one of the most powerful tools at your disposal for supporting your highest aspirations in life.

Denise Hart said, to get what you want in life, you must develop the ability to think in a way that will support your goals and dreams. When you master your mind, you master your life. Motivation makes things happen. What are you planting in your mind?

> **P**urpose & peace?
> **L**ove?
> **A**ppreciation?
> **N**ewness?
> **T**ruth?

What are you planting with, and who are your companions? Good companions to grow alongside are people that will offer time, advice, and support you with decision making. Also, just simply being there. Make sure you also do your part and help others when they are in need. Putting in a little time and effort will pay off in the long run.

Are you the gardener of your mind? Or have you let others plant for you? As they don't understand your vision and purpose, the garden has become overgrown and messy. There is chaos and disorder. The ground may eventually become hard. What you originally planted is not bearing fruit. You are in survival mode and have become unproductive. However, dead things can be revitalised.

Take Action

- Do not let others trespass onto your garden.
- You are entitled to prune or remove anything that encroaches onto your side of the boundary.
- Give your seeds the right amount of heat, light and moisture, and they will germinate successfully.
- What you plant now you can harvest later, if you don't give up.

What are you planting?

Eliminate self-sabotage

Get out of your own way. Remove the roadblocks that are holding you back. Reprogramme your mind so you can live the life you desire. Are there some things that you need to serve notice to?

This is a warning. The limits we put on ourselves can keep us in our comfort zones. This where we feel safe and in control. Serve notice to your limitations today. We are no longer going to be restrained. Stop holding yourself hostage, reframe your limiting beliefs, and turn off the limitations. Some things need to be broken so you can have a breakthrough in your life.

When you step outside your comfort zone, yes it will feel scary. However, once you keep taking those steps, it will start to feel easier. Face your fears and venture out and experience personal growth. When you are in your comfort zone, your brain doesn't want anything to change. However, living outside your comfort zone creates just enough good stress to ramp up your focus, creativity, pace, and drive, and it helps you respond to life stress when unexpected things happen.

There are steps you can take to live outside your comfort zone.

- Don't take the safe choice.
- Consider other points of view.
- Do what you are afraid of.
- Remember that tomorrow is another day.

When I took a leap and gave up my job to become a personal development coach, speaker, and author, it was scary. Each day I would do something that scared me. I still take those steps and push myself. I have realised the benefits of living outside my comfort zone. Here are four reasons why living outside your comfort zone is beneficial:

- Personal growth.
- New challenges and experiences rewire your brain and make it more adaptable, stronger, and healthier.
- You will boost your self-confidence.
- Each milestone makes it easier to tackle another milestone.

Take that step today, just do it. You'll be glad you did. Are you living outside your comfort zone?

What will you do today that scares you?

A key tool that helped me achieve my goals was managing my internal dialogue. This important internal system needs managing because how we speak to ourselves can influence the outcomes in our life.

Reject & replace is something I often use. If a negative word comes to mind, I reject it & replace it with a positive word. This is a fantastic tool to put in your toolbox. Using this tool has helped me to use more positive words. *"There is life and death in the power of the tongue,"* - Proverbs 18:21.

Negative words can be very damaging. When you speak positively it can impact your self-confidence and performance. What word can you reject and replace to better manage your internal dialogue?

Don't be a victim of negative self-talk. Remember, you are listening.

Say goodbye to the *old* you. Say goodbye to limitations because they are stopping you. It can be like a poison; it is stopping you from achieving the happiness you want in your life. Do *you* need to get out of your *own* way?

Seek the help of others

No more lone ranger, trying to make it happen on your own. Hire a coach or a mentor. This is important because you can't see the full picture when you're in the frame. Invest in yourself and be accountable. Most people fail because they don't know yet think they know. Einstein said we cannot solve our problems with the same thinking we used to create them. If you want to get further, get help. You ask not because you are weak, but you want to remain strong. Don't stop until you get the help you need.

Find yourself a coach. A coach is someone who will have the courage to tell you what you need to hear, not what you want to hear. I have been mentored by some great people, Les Brown, Jon Talarico, Lisa Chee and many others. Why? Because I want to improve. They stretched and challenged me and didn't accept excuses. They encouraged me to keep on going.

You are more than you think you are. Having a coach will empower, educate and energise you. They help you get a greater vision of yourself. Have you ever had someone see something in you that you didn't see yourself? That is what a coach does. They will see things in you, give you a vision for yourself beyond your circumstances, job and where you are right now.

Coaching brings about more of you than what you are expressing – things you don't even realise. Because of the encouragement of my coaches I went further than I could have imagined. When I was younger, I was counted out, told I would amount to nothing. I lacked confidence and had low self-esteem. But because of the encouragement of my coach, mentors, parents and husband, I accomplished things far beyond what I had imagined. I had a career of 15 years as a lecturer, became a best-selling author, a personal development coach with a global company. A motivational speaker, with the privilege of speaking all around the world virtually. I wrote a Health and Social Care degree for Sheffield Hallam University.

I state some of my achievements to let you see what's possible when you have the support and encouragement of others. I encourage you to live your life full and die empty, there is more in you right now. Jon Rohn said your life does not get better by chance, it gets better by change.

Surround yourself with like-minded people

In the words of Les Brown, be around 'OQP' - only quality people. A question I often ask people is, 'who is in your circle?' Evaluate who you have around you. It does not have to be a massive support network. However, you need like-minded people around you to give you advice, support and guidance.

Surround yourself with positive people. Spend quality time with them. You become like those you keep close. Look around at your inner circle of friends. Are they who you would like to become? Do you admire and respect them? Surround yourself with positive people who are going to push you to your greatness. *"Iron sharpens iron,"* Proverbs 27:17.

Don't settle for a mediocre mindset. Tell that committee in your mind to shut up and sit down. No more board meetings in your mind and coming into agreement with the negativity. As you work on your mindset, you have to get rid of certain behaviours.

Get rid of the clutter and the unnecessary junk that is clouding your judgement and organise and plan your life. Take charge of your life. As you step into your new mindset, plan it, have a crystal-clear vision for your life. Then, see it, visualise it, get ready to level up your mindset. Finally, anticipate it, believe and you will achieve.

Your mindset matters regardless of the challenges. You have to win in order to have a winning mindset.

Reset your mind with renewed motivation and be consistent in your actions. No more procrastination. Follow the SUCCESS mindset formula. These 7 simple ideas can bring you great power, if you use them to your advantage.

Having a SUCCESS mindset is really no more challenging than not having an unsuccessful mindset. Both require specific actions and attitudes applied consistently over a period of time. Make some changes today and give yourself the gift of success.

Action Steps

1. Stop that stinking thinking
2. Use a morning routine
3. Cultivate an attitude of gratitude
4. Create a motivation mindset
5. Eliminate self-sabotage
6. Seek the help of others
7. Surround yourself with like-minded people

My Notes

PLAN IT. SEE IT. ANTICIPATE IT

Take Action Today

"Action is the foundational key to all success."

- Pablo Picasso

Take action now. There is no time like the present. Plan it. See it. Anticipate it. Commit to putting in the work in order to achieve your goals. Block out dedicated time and become unavailable. Wake up earlier and continue to take action and stay committed.

Having a winning mindset for success will allow you to make things possible. Negative thoughts are no longer permitted to take up space in your mind because it is not in alignment with who you are.

Committed action is a step-by-step process of acting to create a life of integrity, true to one's deepest wishes and longings. Martin Luther King wanted to see change: "I have a dream". That speech was delivered frequently. In order to see change, it takes a committed action.

In order for me to serve my clients, I had to take a committed action. Strolling to my goals will not bring about the desired outcomes I want to see in the timeframe I have set. I have to take charge.

What are you doing to take committed action to reach your goals?

Plan it. See it. Anticipate it

What's next? Have you heard people use that term? Instead, say, what do I need to do *now* to see change in my life?

Here are some productivity tips to support you in completing your tasks.

PRODUCTIVITY TIPS

4 productivity tips that will help you to get things done.

(5) Think about tomorrow, today. At the end of today, write down the one thing you will complete tomorrow. You will wake up in the morning with the day's vision. All that's left is to focus. Sometimes it's the simplest frameworks that help us the most.

(6) Block out your own focus time to boost productivity. Focus time is critical for me to make progress on my projects, but with so many distractions during a typical day, I put my phone on aeroplane mode and get on with the tasks ahead.

(7) Analyse the task list. Now it's time to go through your list, review each task, and decide what you want to do with it. You have four options:
Do: complete the task now
Defer: complete it later
Delegate: assign it to someone else
Delete: remove it from your list

(8) Reward yourself for finishing a big task. To stay motivated for whatever you do, reward yourself. Keep track of your small wins and milestones and celebrate them. So whenever you struggle about your progress, you see how far you've come!

Action Steps

1. Ensure that you take action today to prevent procrastination.
2. Make a commitment to your commitments.
3. Put in the hard work and be consistent.
4. Use the productivity tips so you can get the most out of your day.

Tarnya Coley

My Notes

PLAN IT. SEE IT. ANTICIPATE IT

For the Future

Continue to plan it, see it, and anticipate it. This PSA method will help you win every single time with your goals and achieve them. Now that you have the tools, it is imperative that you use them. I liken it unto an axe. If you do not sharpen your axe, it will become blunt and ineffective. However, sharpen the axe each day if you want lasting results. You must use these tools daily. Repetition is key.

All the best with planning and achieving your goals. Your strongest muscle and your worst enemy is your mind, so train it well. Research suggests that we have about 70,000 thoughts per day. That's 70,000 chances to build yourself up or break yourself down. The conversations that we have with ourselves can have a profound effect on our lives.

If you want to reach your greatest potential it's important to build your mental muscle. Exercise your brain every day and over time, you'll train your brain for happiness and success. Are you ready to level up your mindset?

Five Days to Change Your Mind

Lifetime Guarantee

Whenever you're ready, here are some ways we can work together. Sign up for the FREE five-day mindset challenge.

In this current climate, it is imperative to have the right mindset to focus and achieve your goals. Keep a positive mindset by using the seven useful tools I will present in the five-day mindset challenge.

It's time to develop a positive mindset and continue to stay positive so you can form healthy habits. Join me on the five-day mindset FREE challenge and I will show you how to develop a healthy mindset.

It will allow you to have a positive outlook on life and the way you view your circumstances will change.

It will inspire you to speak and think positively and until it becomes a habit. Then speaking positively becomes a lifestyle.

Benefits of the five-day challenge:

- Lift your mood.
- Improve your phycological and physical well-being.
- Lower depression.

- Relive stress.

Take the five-day mindset challenge, I dare you.

- It is easy to apply these mindset steps.
- You will feel great and your mood will be lifted.
- If you don't take the challenge, you may regret it.
- Today is the day things change.

I have the ultimate level of confidence that this challenge will leave you motivated and inspired.

Eliminate the urge to retreat to your comfort zone.

In just five days this challenge will transform your mindset!

Join the Mindset challenge, register today:
https://tarnya.systeme.io/mindset

My client in Iowa had a goal that she set herself. She had lost hope in achieving it because she disqualified herself and constantly worried about what people would think. Together, we set the goals that she wanted to achieve. We wrote down a plan of action, this was her roadmap for the journey ahead. Then we went on a mindset journey. No more agreeing with the lies and only getting so far. She made a decision that it was her time to achieve her goals. Her strongest desire was to write a poetry book and insert the pictures that she took, as she is a keen photographer. If you believe, you will achieve. She believed that it was possible, and she took immediate action.

Months later, this was a different person I was seeing. She had a coherent plan, crystal clear vision. And believed that she will have her book on Amazon. Six months later, her book is now available on Amazon. My client is now working on her second book. Imagine what you could achieve if you only believed.

Plan it. See it. Anticipate it

Join the Mindset challenge, register today:
https://tarnya.systeme.io/mindset

Last Word

Thank you for reading this book and I hope that you found it useful. Love this book? Don't forget to leave a review! Every review matters, and it matters a *lot!* Head over to Amazon to leave a review for me. Thank you so much.

Follow Tarnya on:

Facebook: https://www.facebook.com/onlinecoachvip

LinkedIn:
https://www.linkedin.com/in/tarnya-coley/

Instagram: https://www.instagram.com/tarnya_coley

If you found this book useful, please consider leaving a short review on Amazon to help other readers know what the book is about and how it can help them.

Craving more?

'Great Goal planner! It helps you to break down those bigger goals and chunking them into smaller manageable steps.' Reader

'Awesome book. A to Z of affirmations for greatness. Love it.'- Reader

Plan it. See it. Anticipate it

Amazon Best-Seller

'An excellent read. Inspiring and heart wrenching. A must for anyone who is on a journey to be the best they can be.'- Reader

About the Author

Tarnya resides in England with her husband and children and is growing a successful global coaching and speaking business. She is a Les Brown certified speaker and has over 18 years' experience speaking on many platforms.

Tarnya is a self-published author of several books. She writes non-fiction books on mindset and goal setting. She has a passion to share her knowledge with the world to make radical mindset shifts.

Dispensing her keys to success has resulted in transforming hundreds of women's lives.

Tarnya's photo kindly taken by Aga Mortlock

Printed in Great Britain
by Amazon